Changes in the structure of employment with economic development

A. S. Oberai

Second edition

This study was carried out with the financial support of the United Nations Fund for Population Activities (UNFPA).

International Labour Office Geneva

ISBN 92-2-102773-2

First published 1978
Second edition 1981

The designations employed in ILO publications, which are in conformity with United Nations practice, and the presentation of material therein do not imply the expression of any opinion whatsoever on the part of the International Labour Office concerning the legal status of any country or territory or of its authorities, or concerning the delimitation of its frontiers.
The responsibility for opinions expressed in signed articles, studies and other contributions rests solely with their authors, and publication does not constitute an endorsement by the International Labour Office of the opinions expressed in them.

ILO publications can be obtained through major booksellers or ILO local offices in many countries, or direct from ILO Publications, International Labour Office, CH-1211 Geneva 22, Switzerland. A catalogue or list of new publications will be sent free of charge from the above address.

Printed by the International Labour Office, Geneva, Switzerland

Table of Contents

I. Introduction

The process of economic development is generally associated with changes in the structure of employment and labour force, and notably with a shift from the traditional to the modern sector activities. The knowledge of the size and structure of employment in the modern sector of a country provides insight into the level and nature of its economic development.

The modern sector is characterised by the production of goods and services for the market. The supply and demand for labour are organised by the mechanism of a labour market, and work relationships are not governed by family or kinship ties. Some of the salient economic features of the modern sector include wage-earning employment, a high wage level and a high level of productivity.[1] In contrast, economic organisation in the traditional sector is characterised by family or household enterprise. Subsistence farming, handicrafts and a variety of unorganised services make up a major segment of the traditional sector.

The purpose of this study is twofold. First, to examine the nature and determinants of structural changes in employment during the course of economic development, differentiating modern from the traditional sector activities. Second, to assess the implications of these changes for a developing economy.

Methodology

The analysis is based on the labour force and wage-employment data available from the censuses for

---

[1] See for example, K.C. Doctor and Hans Gallis: "Modern sector employment in Asian countries: some empirical estimates", in International Labour Review (Geneva, ILO), Dec. 1964.

1960 and 1970 from 51 countries.[1] Although in some cases the data were not available for 1960 and 1970, the data closest to these two years were selected to improve comparability.

The wage-earning employment is taken as a first approximation of the modern sector employment. This approximation is then modified to exclude wage-earners in traditional activities.[2] The total employment, as well as the wage-employment, is disaggregated on the basis of occupation and industry to examine how the process of economic development is likely to redistribute the total labour force and the total volume of wage-employment among different economic sectors and occupational groups.

The per capita GDP is used as a general index of the level of economic development.[3] But other factors

---

[1] The data on labour force and wage-employment by economic sectors, occupational groups and job status were taken from the ILO Year Book of Labour Statistics, (i) all socialist and planned economies were excluded because of differences in concept and definitions of the variables. (ii) The concepts and other data sources are discussed in appendices A and B. (iii) The sample of countries with data on the GDP per capita is given in appendix C.

[2] The modern sector employment is defined as the sum of all professional, administrative, clerical workers and wage-earners among sales, mining, transport and production process workers. See appendix A for definitions and estimations of the modern sector and wage-employment.

[3] See for example, I. Adelman and C. Morris: Society, politics and economic development (Baltimore, Johns Hopkins University Press, 1967). The authors have shown through factor analysis that many economic and social phenomena are systematically related to the level of income and, hence, the per capita GDP can serve as a general index of development.

such as population and labour force growth, changes in the rural-urban composition of population, and the size and structure of exports are also considered to be influencing the level and structure of wage-employment.

The hypotheses which are tested include the following:

(1) In the process of economic development, there is a tendency for the labour force to shift to economic sectors and occupational groups characterised by high wage-labour requirements;

(2) The share of wage-employment in the total employment continues to rise in an economy until a level of economic advancement is attained beyond which there is no appreciable increase in the relative share of wage-employment. In other words, there is a non-proportional relation between the share of wage-employment and economic growth;

(3) The rise in the over-all wage-employment ratio in an economy is associated with changes in the distribution of the total wage-employment among economic sectors. For example, the proportion of wage-earners increases in both secondary and tertiary sectors and declines in the primary sector with an over-all increase in the wage-employment ratio;

(4) In a developing economy, the growth in the share of modern sector employment in the total employment is inversely related to the over-all rate of growth of the labour force. This may be due to factors, both of demand and supply. On the one hand, the relatively slow growth of employment in the modern sector may result from the sluggish growth in demand for the modern sector goods, the adoption of capital-intensive techniques, and the prevalent high-wage rates. On the other hand, the excessive supply of labour may result in a more rapid expansion of the traditional sector which has a higher labour absorptive capacity due both to free entry and more flexible wage-rates;

(5) The size and structure of exports have a direct influence on the level and structure of employment in an economy. Both the modern sector and wage-employment are a positive function of exports and the shift from the traditional to the modern sector employment is greater when the growth in exports is accompanied with changes in the composition of exports;

(6) Among other factors, the rate of urbanisation and the rising income levels are positively correlated with the growth in the share of modern sector employment in the total employment. Since the pattern of demand of the urban population is generally biased in favour of non-agricultural commodities, and the income elasticity of demand for these products is generally greater than that for agricultural commodities, the increasing urbanisation leads to an increase in the share of the non-agricultural sectors in the gross domestic product, and thereby shifts employment from the traditional sector to the modern sector.

II. Determinants of Structural Changes in Employment

Before we look at shifts in the sectoral and occupational distribution of the labour force and wage-employment with economic development, we shall briefly consider the factors which may cause such a shift. While examining the structure of production, Fisher and Clark observed a progression in the allocation of labour from primary to secondary to tertiary employment, which they explained largely on the basis of changes in domestic demand (hereafter referred to as the C-F hypothesis).[1]

---

[1] The changes in the industrial distribution of the labour force and employment are said to have been observed first by Petty in the seventeenth century. See, for instance, A.G.B. Fisher: "Production, primary, secondary and tertiary", in Economic Record, June 1939; C. Clark: The conditions of economic progress (London, Macmillan, 1940 (2nd edn., 1951, 3rd edn., 1957)).

The C-F hypothesis is, in essence, a theory of the determination of sectoral output, linked to an observed regularity in the movement of sectoral employment, assuming that output patterns determine employment patterns.[1]

But this argument is primarily demand-centred, relying largely on income effects. The sequence in sectoral employment shifts is normally explained as follows. The per capita income determines the pattern of consumption in accordance with sectoral income elasticities of demand (Engel's law); the pattern of consumption, in turn, determines the pattern of sectoral output; and the pattern of sectoral output itself determines the pattern of sectoral employment. However, the hypothesis ignores or assumes away effects on output arising from prices, substitutability in consumer preferences resulting from relative price changes, sectoral differences in the relative growth of factor supplies. Consequently, the C-F hypothesis fails to predict the contrary movements of output and employment in the secondary and tertiary sectors. For instance, Ramos in a recent study of several Latin American countries observed a strong shift in employment from the primary into the tertiary sector, bypassing the secondary sector.[2]

According to Ramos, this inadequacy in the C-F hypothesis may stem from two factors. On the one hand, differentials in the growth of sectoral output may

---

[1] See Joseph R. Ramos: Labour and development in Latin America (New York, Columbia University Press, 1970).

[2] Ibid., p. 141. For similar conclusions see G.B. Rodgers, R. Wéry and M.J.D. Hopkins: Economic-demographic modelling for development planning: BACHUE-Philippines (Geneva, ILO, 1976; mimeographed World Employment Programme research working paper; restricted).

not correspond to sectoral differentials in income elasticity of demand, and, on the other hand, the sectoral employment may not increase in proportion to the sectoral output.

The non-proportional relationship of sectoral output and sectoral employment may be due to several reasons. First, there may be sectoral differentials in factor intensity. Generally, the manufacturing production is more capital-intensive than tertiary production. As a result, an increase in the manufacturing output will provide less additional employment than a similar increase in the output of the tertiary sector. Second, there may exist differentials in sectoral elasticities of factor substitution. The greater the sectoral elasticity of factor substitution, the greater will be the extent of substitution of capital for labour in that sector. In their famous article, Arrow, Chenery, Minhas and Solow have shown that the elasticity of substitution between capital and labour is greatest in the primary sector, and least in the tertiary sector.[1] Therefore an increase in the proportion of capital to labour will induce the greatest substitution of capital for labour in the primary sector, and least in the tertiary sector, with the result that employment with a unit increase in output will decrease most in the primary sector, and increase most in the tertiary sector. Third, there may also be sectoral differentials in the rates of technological growth. Assuming technological growth to be factor-neutral, the greater a sector's rate

---

[1] K. Arrow, H. Chenery, B. Minhas and R. Solow: "Capital labour substitution and economic efficiency", in Review of Economics and Statistics, August 1961. Their estimates of the elasticity of substitution between capital and labour for different sectors of the economy, from data on relative factor inputs and prices in Japan and the United States were:

b = 1.15 for agriculture, mining, paper and non-ferrous metals;
= 0.9 for manufacturing;
= 0.4 for personal services.

of technological growth, the slower will be its growth of employment with a unit increase in output. The most common view is that the rate of technological growth is lowest for the tertiary sector and highest for the primary and secondary sectors.[1] This would result, *ceteris paribus*, in a more rapid rate of absorption of labour per unit of growth in output in the tertiary sector, and a correspondingly slower rate of labour absorption in the primary and secondary sectors.

Thus the observed non-proportionality of sectoral employment and output requires that the analysis be extended to include other factors. Kuznets, Chenery and several others have advocated the need for a more comprehensive treatment of both demand and supply factors in seeking to explain the patterns of sectoral employment.[2] The changes in the composition of production, together with the available technology, determine the changes in the demand for labour. The low income elasticity of demand for food and primary products implies a shift in demand away from these goods as the level of income rises, whereas the demand for less essential manufactured goods and services is likely to account for an increasing proportion of income. Factors affecting the supply of labour include the growth of population, its distribution between rural and urban areas, and the levels of education.

---

[1] First, the tertiary production is typically small-scale. The benefits of innovation accrue only fractionally to the innovator, since his share of the over-all market for the product is apt to be small. Second, much of the tertiary production cannot be traded; hence it is less subject to the stimulus of competition for innovation, and has a small market.

[2] See for example, S. Kuznets: *Modern economic growth: rate, structure and spread* (Yale University Press, 1966); Hollis Chenery and Moises Syrquin: *Patterns of development 1950-1970* (Oxford University Press, 1975).

The interaction of supply and demand determines the distribution of labour as well as differences in labour productivity and income among economic sectors. In his recent study, Chenery has argued that if all sectors had the same production functions, factor prices and entry conditions, we would expect the changes in the pattern of employment to follow closely the pattern of structural changes in output.[1] Chenery observes, however, that there are systematic differences between the two patterns. This may be due to a number of factors. First, the demand for labour grows more rapidly in the urban areas. Second, immobility and unequal access to capital and other factors makes it difficult to equalise factor returns. Third, the technological growth is more concentrated in the modern branches of each sector. And finally, the unprecedented growth of the labour force in recent years has greatly exceeded the growth of demand in the modern sector of most economies.

However, Chenery's observations require a detailed study on the relationship between changes in employment and output among economic sectors in a developing economy.[2] In section III, we shall examine the relative growth of employment in secondary and tertiary sectors and see if there are any marked differences in the pattern of employment growth in these sectors. In the subsequent sections we shall also look at the possible effects of the rate of growth of the labour force, and the rural-urban composition of population on the level and growth of the modern sector employment, and see how the process of urbanisation alters the occupational distribution of the labour force through the spread of education and cultural aspirations.

---

[1] See Chenery and Syrquin, 1975, op. cit.

[2] The lack of data on output by economic sectors imposes a limitation on our analysis of the detailed study of the relationship between changes in employment and output.

III. Economic Development and Changes in the Sectoral Distribution of the Labour Force and Wage-employment

The process of economic development is associated with a change in the distribution of the labour force among economic sectors. But it is not merely the sectoral distribution of the labour force that is likely to change over time. The sectoral distribution of wage-employment also changes during the course of economic development.[1]

To analyse these changes, we have grouped countries into three levels of economic development (low, medium and high) on the basis of GDP per capita in 1960.[2] Wage-employment in each sector is expressed as a proportion of the total wage-employment in the economy. Then for each sector, the averages are computed for each group of countries.[3] Similar ratios are then computed for the same groups of countries for 1970. The comparison between 1960 and 1970 figures in table 1 illustrates the inter-temporal shift in the sectoral distribution of wage-employment.

For group I countries in 1960, agriculture appears to be the most important industry in terms of wage-labour

---

[1] See for example, Teshome Mulat: "The changes in the level and structure of employment in developing countries", Ph.D. thesis, University of Manchester, 1971.

[2] We have selected countries with GDP per capita less than \$300 to be in group I. Those with GDP per capita between \$300 and \$700 to constitute group II and with GDP per capita greater than \$700 to be in group III. See appendix C.

[3] The census data for sectoral distribution of the labour force and wage-employment in 1960 and 1970 are taken from the ILO _Year Book of Labour Statistics_ (table 2A), for various years.

Table 1: Percentage distribution of wage-employment by economic sectors for 1960 and 1970[1]

Group	Sample size	GDP per capita US$	Percentages					
			Agriculture, forestry, hunting and fishing	Mining and quarrying	Manufac- turing	Construc- tion	Transport	Services
1960								
I	19	196	37	4	13	7	5	30
II	10	447	14	1	23	9	7	43
III	13	1,656	5	2	33	10	8	40
1970								
I	19	322	31	1	17	8	5	34
II	10	992	9	1	25	10	7	46
III	13	2,890	4	1	31	10	7	45

1 (i) Each group in 1970 has exactly the same countries as in 1960 in order to observe the shift in the share of sectoral distribution of wage-employment over time.

(ii) The row totals do not add up to 100 due to the exclusion of the unemployed and the activities not adequately described.

(iii) The GDP per capita is in constant prices.

absorption, followed closely by services.[1] On average, about 37 per cent and 30 per cent of wage-employment is found in agriculture and services respectively. Manufacturing is not a particularly important source of wage-employment and accounts for only 13 per cent of the total wage-employment. Between 1960 and 1970, the combined shares of agriculture and mining declined (from 41 to 32 per cent), whereas the shares of manufacturing and services increased in total wage-employment.

For group II countries, services rank highest as a source of wage-employment followed closely by manufacturing. Moreover, the manufacturing and service sectors display the greatest increase in the proportion of wage-employment as a country advances from a low to medium level of development. Equally marked is the decline in the percentage of wage-employment in agriculture between group I and group II countries. Looking at the changes between 1960 and 1970 for group II countries, the percentage of wage-employment in agriculture declined from 14 to 9 per cent, whereas in manufacturing and services it increased considerably.

In the case of group III countries, manufacturing is an important sector, absorbing about 33 per cent of the total wage-employment in 1960. However, services, which include commerce, electricity, gas and water, constitute the principal sector and account for 40 per cent of wage-employment. Considering the changes between 1960 and 1970, the shares of agriculture, construction and transport in wage-employment are largely unchanged, whereas wage-employment in manufacturing declines slightly and the service sector wage-employment rises from 40 to 45 per cent.

---

[1] Services include: (i) electricity, gas and water; (ii) wholesale and retail trade; (iii) financing, insurance and business services; (iv) community, social and personal services; (v) sanitary services, etc. All services have been grouped together because of the differences in old and new international standard industrial classifications (ISIC).

It is also interesting to note from the comparison between group II and group III countries for 1970 that construction, transport and services account for approximately the same proportion of wage-employment, although there are notable differences in wage-employment absorption in manufacturing and agriculture. The share of agriculture in wage-employment for group II countries is 5 per cent higher, and that of manufacturing is 6 per cent lower than that for group III countries.[1]

The intersectoral redistribution of wage-employment may be restated by utilising a simplified classification of primary, secondary and tertiary sectors. The primary sector includes agriculture, forestry, hunting and fishing. The secondary sector includes mining and quarrying, manufacturing and construction. The remaining industries, such as electricity, gas, water and sanitary services, commerce, transport, and storage and communications form the tertiary sector. This three-sector classification is useful for purposes of extracting some generalisations on sectoral changes in the distribution of wage-employment at different levels of industrial and economic development. Wage-employment and the labour force distributions among primary, secondary and tertiary sectors are given in table 2.

It is clear that primary employment declines during the course of economic development with respect to all groups of countries. Since the primary sector's share in the over-all wage-employment falls as per capita income rises, the percentage share of the secondary and tertiary sectors together increases. However, the issue is not whether wage-employment increases in the secondary and tertiary sectors combined, but whether there is any systematic pattern of change. Does the secondary

---

[1] But the comparison is valid only as a first approximation. Since the countries have been grouped on the basis of GDP per capita in 1960, not all countries in group II have GDP per capita less than US$700. In fact, the mean GDP per capita for group II countries in 1970 has risen to 992.

Table 2: Percentage distribution of labour force and wage-employment among major economic sectors for 1960 and 1970*

Group	Wage-employment (%)			Labour force (%)		
	Primary	Secondary	Tertiary	Primary	Secondary	Tertiary
1960						
I	37	24	35	60	14	21
II	14	33	50	29	26	41
III	5	45	48	14	39	45
1970						
I	31	26	39	49	18	28
II	9	36	53	22	29	45
III	4	42	52	11	35	51

* The row totals do not add up to 100 due to the exclusion of the unemployed and the activities not adequately described.

employment rise more rapidly than the tertiary employment, or do both rise at the same rate, or is there, in fact, no pattern at all?

The data for 1960 in table 2 indicate that between group I and group II countries, the share of the tertiary sector in the total wage-employment (as well as in the labour force) rises much faster than does the share of the secondary sector. The share of the primary sector in the total wage-employment appears to have declined by about 23 per cent, whereas for the secondary and tertiary sectors, it increased by 9 and 15 per cent respectively. Also for both these groups of countries, the same pattern is observed when we examine the changes that occur between 1960 and 1970. However, between group II and group III countries, the share of the tertiary sector in the total wage-employment declined moderately, whereas in the primary sector it continued to decline rapidly. The entire decline in the primary and tertiary sectors is captured by the secondary sector in which the sectoral share of the total wage-employment increased from 33 to 45 per cent. With respect to changes in the distribution of the labour force between group II and group III countries, the share of the tertiary sector in the total labour force appears to rise, although the increase is far less dramatic than the increase in the secondary sector.

The data, therefore, suggest that the decline of the wage-employment in the primary sector in the early stages of development is mainly absorbed in tertiary employment. A relatively greater increase in the proportion of wage-employment (and the labour force) in the tertiary sector is also revealed over time for group I and group II countries. This may be due to a number of factors. First, the expansion of economic and social infrastructure implies an early rise in tertiary employment. Public institutions (schools, police, hospitals, etc.) and the public operation of economic enterprises (e.g. public works, post, railways, etc.) in the early stages of economic development account for high volumes of wage-employment. Second, the tendency for a growing proportion of the labour force to be employed in the tertiary sector may be due to its low elasticity of factor substitution, its slow rate of technological growth and the likely shift of output within the tertiary sector toward its unskilled labour intensive subsectors of production.[1] Third, there is an employment multiplier

---

[1] A relatively slower expansion of the secondary sector seems largely because of the increasingly capital-intensive nature of manufacturing. Ramos observes that during the 1960s many Latin American countries had concentrated their investment in manufacturing, particularly in heavy industry, without regard to employment considerations and the "manufacturing output rose

associated with the growth of secondary (mainly manufacturing) output. The growth of the modern industrial structure requires the expansion of commercial and government services so that an increase in secondary output and employment generates multiples of that increase in the tertiary output and employment.

But it is interesting to note that once a certain stage of development has been reached, the tertiary sector's share in the over-all wage-employment stabilises and even declines somewhat (from group II to group III, as reflected in table 2) whereas the wage-employment in the secondary sector continues to rise. This may be due to several reasons. First, the tertiary employment starts from a relatively higher base and expands more quickly in the early stages of economic development so that further growth is less likely. Second, the tertiary and secondary sectors differ in their wage-labour requirements. The tertiary employment contains relatively high proportions of self- and family-employment even at high levels of industrial development because of the persistence of tradition where many trade and other service activities are left self- or family-owned and managed. Third, at the higher levels of development the demand for manufactured goods grows faster than tertiary products and accounts for an increasing proportion of income.

Table 2 also shows that, in general, irrespective of the level of economic development attained, the tertiary employment accounts for the largest proportion of wage-employment.[1]

---

strongly but without commensurate increases in manufacturing employment". See Joseph R. Ramos: op. cit., p. 129. Also see Mayrar, Frankman and Charle: "Employment in the service sector in sub-Saharan Africa", in Journal of Modern Studies, Vol. 11, No. 2, June 1973.

[1] The sole exception is for group I countries in 1960. However, the 2 per cent difference between primary and tertiary wage-employment is certainly within the realm of statistical error.

Although the data indicate a broad association between the level of economic development and the sectoral distribution of the labour force and wage-employment, the use of generalised classification for reasons of exposition may have oversimplified our analysis. For the purposes of policy considerations, however, more detailed information on employment shifts is required. Shifts in wage-employment and labour force may occur within the particular industries of an economic sector as it does between economic sectors. The study of these structural changes is particularly important for understanding the dynamics of labour markets and their adjustments.

We have also computed wage employment in a sector as a ratio of the total employment in that sector. The mean values of this sectoral wage-employment ratio for each group of countries, and for each economic sector are given in table 3.

Table 3: Wage-employment as a percentage of total sectoral employment for 1960 and 1970

Group	Agriculture, forestry, hunting, fishing, etc.	Mining and quarrying	Manufacturing	Construction	Transport	Services
1960						
I	31	86	60	87	81	65
II	28	87	76	81	80	75
III	34	97	91	85	89	83
1970						
I	32	85	69	85	78	67
II	27	88	82	78	79	78
III	33	95	91	83	89	82

Table 3 shows that the sectoral wage-employment ratio is a rising function of the level of economic development in the case of mining and quarrying, manufacturing and services, whereas in agriculture (1960 and 1970), construction (1960 and 1970) and transport (1960), there is some indication of decreasing wage-employment during the early stages and increasing during the later stages of development.[1] However, there is no uniform pattern observed with respect to the rise in the wage-employment ratio from group I to group III countries in all economic sectors (in construction, there is even a slight decline). The rise is relatively more marked in manufacturing and services than in other sectors. But the data suggest that within each sector, shifts from less productive to more productive lines of activity are an important feature of the growth process. In agriculture, there is a shift from the traditional subsistence farming to the modernised and more specialised commercial farming; in manufacturing, from handi-

---

1

For example, wage-employment in agriculture can decline during the early stages of development if the manpower previously available for wage-employment now remains confined to their own farms as self-employed and unpaid family helpers to meet the increased demand for labour resulting from improvement in the irrigation infrastructure, the use of high-yielding varieties and the increase in cropping intensity. The transition from stage 2 to stage 3 may be explained by the increasing use of mechanical power and machinery, and dependence on hired labour.

While such a U-shaped relationship can arise, a careful check on the data indicates that this is due to the inclusion of Greece and Japan among group II countries. These two countries have reported a low percentage of wage-employment in agriculture because of the exclusion of paid family workers from the group "wage and salary earners". When these two countries are excluded, the mean percentage wage-employment in agriculture in 1960 and 1970 is about 33 per cent and 32 per cent respectively.

crafts, and cottage industries to mechanised factories of increasing scale; and in transport, from human and animal carriers to mechanised vehicles. Thus the process of industrialisation and economic growth alters the labour force status distribution in favour of wage-employment (i.e. the proportions of self- and family-employment diminishes) in most of the economic sectors, as well as in the economy as a whole.

As between 1960 and 1970, we find the share of wage-employment falling in group I for mining and quarrying, construction and transport; in group II for agriculture, construction and transport; and in group III for all sectors, except manufacturing and transport, in the case of which it is stable. It should be pointed out, however, that the decreases are relatively small, whereas the increases, mainly in manufacturing and services for groups I and II, are quite substantial.

Table 3 also shows the difference between the economic sectors in relative wage-labour requirements. Specifically, the agricultural sector contains the smallest proportion of wage-employment (as a ratio of total sectoral employment). This is true irrespective of the level of economic development. It may be concluded that whereas primary employment is consistent with high proportions of self- and family-employment, secondary and tertiary employment is characterised by high wage-employment independent of the level of industrialisation and economic growth.

It is also interesting to look at the wage-labour requirements in the services sector. The total labour force absorbed in this sector is neither demand-induced nor a "residual category".[1] Therefore it is more useful to disaggregate the total services employment into modern (demand-determined) and traditional (supply-determined) components. As a rough approximation, all

---

[1] See, for example, A.S. Bhalla: "The role of services in employment expansion", in <u>International Labour Review</u> (Geneva, ILO), May 1970.

wage-earning and salaried employment may be considered to be modern; whereas all non-wage or self-employed and unpaid family labour may be regarded as traditional.[1] Therefore the share of wage-employment in the total sectoral employment in services can be used as a proxy for the modern services. And the data in table 3 suggest the share of modern services to be rising among the three groups of countries. Over time the share of modern services also rises for groups I and II but then enters a period of stability and decline. However, the increase in the demand for modern services may be partly due to the expansion of economic and social overheads characteristic of the development process. But the decline in the share of traditional service activities despite rapid economic growth warrants further study of the structural changes which occur outside manufacturing, and particularly within the services sector.

IV. Economic Development and Changes in the Occupational Distribution of Labour Force and Wage-employment

A general rise in the level of wage-employment is also associated with occupational distributional changes. The latter, in turn, reflect changes in the quality of the labour force. A rise in the quality of the labour force can be measured by an increase in the proportion of labour force in highly skilled occupational categories.

To examine the changes in the occupational composition of the labour force and wage-employment which accompany economic growth, the following ratios were computed for countries at a relatively low, intermediate and high level of economic development, both for 1960 and 1970:

---

[1] The situation with respect to self-employment in the developing countries is very complex. All self-employment may not be of traditional character. Many professional services, such as those of physicians and lawyers, represent a "modern" element.

(a) wage-earners in each occupation as a percentage of total employment in that occupation;

(b) the proportion of the labour force in each occupation;

(c) wage-employment in each occupation as a percentage of the total wage-employment in the economy.

Wage-earners as a percentage of the total employment in each occupation appears to vary between occupational categories, as illustrated in table 4. Some occupational categories, such as professional, clerical, service, transport and production process workers, have a consistently high proportion of wage-employment, independent of the level of economic development. In contrast, agricultural workers consistently account for less than 50 per cent of the wage-earners in the total employment in that occupation.

Moreover, the status distributional changes that occur during the process of economic development are greater in the case of some occupational categories than in the case of others. Within certain occupational categories, there are notable increases in the proportion of workers in wage or salary employment. For occupational categories such as professional, administrative, agricultural and sales workers, the share of wage-employment rises among the three groups of countries except for professional workers from group I to II in 1960. Over time, the share of wage-employment also rises in these occupations except in the case of agricultural workers in group I where it declines slightly. On the other hand, there is no uniform pattern observed with respect to the rise in the case of clerical and service workers. These two occupations show more or less the same mean proportion of wage-employment over different levels of development.

The occupational distributional changes that are likely to occur during the process of economic development can also be illustrated by examining the changes in the occupational distribution of the total wage-employment,

Table 4: Wage-earners as a percentage of total employment in each occupation for 1960 and 1970

Group	Pro-fessional workers	Adminis-trative workers	Clerical worker	Sales workers	Agricultural workers	Craftsmen, production process, transport workers	Service workers
	(1)	(2)	(3)	(4)	(5)	(6)	(7)
1960							
I	84	55	94	25	31	70	87
II	83	61	98	43	32	82	90
III	88	64	99	60	35	86	87
1970							
I	85	60	96	25	30	70	82
II	86	68	98	50	35	81	87
III	91	79	97	65	41	89	87

[1] Japan and Greece were excluded from group II for the reason cited earlier. See footnote 1, page. 17.

Table 5: Percentage distribution of total wage-employment and labour force by occupations for 1960 and 1970

Category	Group	Professional workers	Administrative workers	Clerical workers	Sales workers	Agricultural workers	Craftsmen, production process, transport workers	Service workers
		(1)	(2)	(3)	(4)	(5)	(6)	(7)
Wage-earners	1960							
	I	5	1	6	3	37	32	13
	II	7	2	11	6	13	41	15
	III	10	3	13	6	6	50	11
	1970							
	I	7	1	10	3	30	34	11
	II	10	2	14	6	9	40	15
	III	13	3	17	7	4	43	11
Labour force	1960							
	I	2	1	3	6	59	18	6
	II	5	2	7	9	30	31	11
	III	9	3	10	8	14	42	10
	1970							
	I	4	1	4	7	50	21	6
	II	7	3	9	9	21	33	12
	III	11	4	14	9	10	38	10

or of the labour force (see table 5). Primary occupational categories account for the largest proportion of the total labour force and the total wage-employment in the case of group I countries. The mean proportion of the labour force in this occupational category is about 60 per cent, and this ratio declines between group II and group III countries. Group III countries have a mean proportion of 14 per cent of the labour force in the primary occupational category in 1960, which further declines to 10 per cent in 1970. In the case of other occupational categories, the proportion of the labour force (in each occupation) rises between the levels of development except in the case of sales and service workers from group II to III, both in 1960 and 1970. The increase in the mean proportions of the labour force in occupational categories 3 (clerical) and 6 (craftsmen, transport, and production process workers) is particularly significant between group I and group III countries.

It is also interesting to note the changes in the rank order of occupational categories as a result of the redistribution of the labour force among occupational groups. For group I and II (developing) countries combined, the major occupational cateogries 5, 6 and 7 are ranked, first, second and third in terms of their respective shares in the total labour force. But in the case of group III countries, the most important occupational categories are 6 and 5 in 1960. But in 1970, where the share of wage-employment has further declined in the case of group III countries, the occupational categories that assume importance are 6, 3 and 1 in that order. It should be noted that the rank order of occupational categories are not the same when we look at the distribution of the total wage-employment except at higher levels of development as in the case of group III countries (see table 5). This is due to the fact that the labour force not only includes wage-earners, but also the self-employed and family workers. Since the distribution of status groups also changes during the process of economic development, the rank order of occupational categories between the labour force and wage-earners is not the same.

The distribution of wage-employment by occupational categories, as shown in table 5, indicates that the percentage of total wage-employment in the primary occupational category declines from 37 per cent to 6 per cent between group I and group III countries, and these proportions decline further over time. For group II and group III countries, the most important occupational category includes craftsmen, transport and production process workers which absorbs about 40 to 50 per cent of the total wage-employment. In the case of service workers, initially, the percentage of the total wage-employment increases and then declines, and stabilises at approximately 11 per cent at higher levels of development.

The changes in the distribution of the labour force (and wage-employment) among occupational categories in the process of economic development can also be restated, using the aggregative classification of occupations. A distinction that is often made is between "white-collar" and "blue-collar" workers. The former includes professional, administrative, clerical and sales workers (occupational categories 1, 2, 3 and 4), whereas the latter includes craftsmen, transport and production process workers (occupational category 6). The remaining occupational categories 5 and 7 are classified as "primary workers". The distribution of the labour force and wage-employment by broad occupational categories is given in table 6. The mean proportion of white-collar workers rises among all the three groups of countries, and also between 1960 and 1970. Also rising with the levels of economic development is the proportion of blue-collar workers. In contrast, the occupational category "primary workers" is characterised by a declining proportion.

Technical, professional and related workers, for example, are likely to increase in the course of development because of the tendency to utilise the increasing numbers of scientists, engineers and technicians as well as other professionals in research activities and in industry. Similarly, the increase in the proportion of administrative, executive and managerial workers can be treated in part as a function of the growth of large-scale organisation of commerce between the levels of economic development. Hence, the rise in the mean proportions of white-collar workers among the three groups of countries and over time.

Table 6: Percentage distribution of labour force and wage-employment among major occupational groups for 1960 and 1970

Group	Labour force (%)			Wage-employment (%)		
	White-collar	Primary	Blue-collar	White-collar	Primary	Blue-collar
1960						
I	12	65	18	15	50	32
II	23	39	31	26	28	41
III	30	24	42	32	17	50
1970						
I	16	56	21	21	41	34
II	28	33	33	32	24	40
III	38	20	38	40	15	43

In order to observe how the movements in the broad occupational groupings are related to movements in per capita income, we estimated the relation between the proportion of the labour force in broad occupational categories and the GDP per capita. Since the occupational composition of the labour force is also determined by independent supply factors such as education, we have included the primary and secondary school enrolment ratio to reflect the general level of education and the possible educational qualities of the labour force in general.[1]

[1] Ideally, we should have used the educational level of the employed labour force if data were available.

Thus the following equation was estimated by ordinary least squares using a log linear specification and the regression results are presented in table 7.[1]

$$\text{Log Li} = a + b \log (Y/N) + c \log E + e$$

where

Li = the percentage of the labour force in white-collar, blue-collar and primary occupations (1960)

Y/N = the GDP per capita in US dollars (1960)

E = primary and secondary school enrolment ratio (1960)

e = error term

The regression results confirm the earlier proposition that the proportion of the labour force in white-collar and blue-collar jobs is positively related to the levels of economic development. The primary and secondary school enrolment ratio is significant at the 5 per cent level for white-collar workers, but fails to be significant for the other two occupational groups. Perhaps this is because the white-collar group includes occupations requiring the highest level of education and training.

There is yet another aspect of occupational distributional changes. It arises from the inter-dependency of occupational and industrial composition of the labour force. Some occupations are, in part, or wholly confined to certain industries, whereas others are found in varying proportions in different industries. This relationship between the occupational and industrial distribution of the labour force is also likely to be

---

[1] The data refer to 1960. The regression results for 1970 were similar and, therefore, are not presented here.

Table 7: Regressions of labour force in major occupational categories on income and education (t values are given in brackets)

Dependent variable per cent of labour force in:	Constant	Regression coeff. (b)	Regression coeff. (c)	R^2	F-value	Sample size
White-collar	-.200	.480** (8.11)	.115** (2.44)	.676	40.610	42
Blue-collar	.063	.471** (7.57)	.058 (1.17)	.607	31.875	42
Primary occupation	2.837	-.433** (9.22)	-.054 (1.42)	.709	47.268	42

** significant at 1 per cent level

modified as a result of increasing diversity of occupational specialisation within industries, reflecting the growing complexity of economic organisation and technology.

A change in the share of a given occupation in the labour force can be considered to be the sum of two components, the effect of any change in the distribution of the labour force among industries (called the "industry effect") and the effect of any change in the occupational composition of the labour force within industries (called the "occupational effect"). Gnanasekaran observed that in the United States the share of professional workers in civilian employment increased from 8.8 per cent in 1950 to 11.8 per cent in 1960. He attributed four-fifths of this change to the industry effect (especially the rapid growth of employment in professional and related service industries) and one-fifth to the occupational effect (especially the increasing share of professional workers in employment within manufacturing, professional and related service industries).[1] However, such an analysis can be misleading unless one recognises that the occupational composition of the labour force and of employment is not determined solely by the factors of demand. There are also independent supply factors, including the extent of education and vocational training which workers receive, and their preferences for different kinds of work. Thus the occupational composition of available manpower may influence the occupation mixes in various industries, as the relative scarcity in the supply of qualified workers in certain occupations may cause capital substitutions and inter-occupational transfers of labour supply. Similarly, the growth of industries may also be significantly affected by the conditions of labour supply in the occupations on which the industries depend.

The analysis of the occupation-industry relationship is beyond the scope of this study since the data are needed on the occupational distribution of labour force by major industries or economic sectors. Nevertheless, the study of the occupation-industry relationship is extremely useful for determining the factors which affect employment opportunities in various occupations, including the effects of changing technology and shifting demand on the products of various industries.

V. Rate of Growth of Labour Force and Modern Sector Employment

In terms of employment, the developing economies are often dualistic. Since the modern sector is often characterised by relatively higher wage rates, there is usually an excess supply of labour available to this sector. Therefore the growth of employment in the

---

[1] K.S. Gnanasekaran: Interrelations between industrial and occupational changes in manpower, United States 1950-1960 (Philadelphia, 1966).

modern sector is primarily determined by the growth in the demand for labour. The traditional sector, on the other hand, is characterised by personalised economic relationships which permit the absorption of labour into economic activities even at very low levels of productivity. Thus the growth of employment in this sector is determined not only by the demand for labour, but also by the supply of labour in the economy as a whole.

When employment rises in both the traditional and modern sectors, it is the differential rate of growth of the modern sector that determines the pace of modernisation of the employment structure. For a given differential rate of growth of the modern sector employment, the lower the initial proportion of the modern sector in the total employment, the slower will be the shift towards a more modern employment structure. Furthermore, if the rate of growth of the labour force exceeds the rate of growth of the demand for labour in the modern sector, the share of the modern sector in the total employment may even decline. This decline may be due to both demand and supply factors. On the one hand, the relatively slow growth of employment in the modern sector may result from the sluggish growth in demand for the modern sector goods, the adoption of capital-intensive techniques, and the prevalent high wage-rates. On the other hand, the excessive supply of labour may result in a more rapid expansion of the traditional sector characterised by a socio-economic structure which permits the absorption of additional workers largely by spreading underemployment.

Thus we hypothesise that given the initial share of the modern sector employment in the total employment, the higher the rate of growth of the labour force, the more difficult it is to absorb the growing labour force in the modern sector and, therefore, to stabilise the proportion of labour force engaged in the traditional sectors. To test this hypothesis we have specified and estimated the following model:

$$M_r = a + b\,Y_r + c\,M_s + d\,LF_r + e$$

where

M_r = the percentage change in the share of the modern sector employment between 1960 and 1970[1]

Y_r = the period rate of growth of GDP between 1960 and 1970

M_s = the percentage modern sector employment in 1960

LF_r = the period rate of growth of the labour force between 1960 and 1970[2]

e = the error term

Two more variables have been included among the independent variables. The rate of growth of GDP is added because of its accelerating effect on the growth of the modern sector employment. The variable M_s is included to control for the size of the modern sector (absorptive capacity), since at the higher levels of development when the modern sector has reached its limits, further increases in the modern sector share are less likely.

1

$$M_r = \left(\frac{M_2 - M_1}{M_1}\right) \times 100$$

where M_2 and M_1 are the percentage shares of the modern sector employment in 1970 and 1960 respectively.

2

$$LF_r = \left(\frac{LF_{70} - LF_{60}}{LF_{60}}\right) \times 100.$$

The model was estimated by using the ordinary least squares. Each independent variable was introduced stepwise to see the change in the size and magnitude of other regression coefficients. Separate regressions were run for both the total sample and a sample of the developing countries

The regression results presented in table 8 indicate that both the level of the modern sector employment and rate of growth of the labour force are inversely related to the period rate of growth of the share of the modern sector employment (see columns 1 and 2). The sign and the magnitude of these coefficients remain relatively stable when the period rate of growth of GDP is included in the equation. The same pattern is observed for both the entire sample and a sample of the developing countries. The elasticities of the period rate of growth of the share of the modern sector employment with respect to each independent variable are given below:

Elasticity		Developing countries	All countries
η_{M_r, LF_r} -	elasticity of growth of the share of the modern sector employment with respect to the growth of the labour force	-0.29	-0.23
$\eta_{M_r, GDP}$ -	elasticity of growth of the share of the modern sector employment with respect to the growth of the GDP	0.40	0.37
η_{M_r, M_s} -	elasticity of growth of the share of the modern sector employment with respect to the level of the modern sector employment	-1.04	-1.79

Table 8: Stepwise regression of growth in modern sector employment on growth of GDP, labour force and level of modern sector employment
(t values are given in brackets)

Variable	Mean value of the variable	All countries Column 1			Mean value of the variable	Developing countries Column 2		
Equation								
Constant		36.11	41.02	36.31		37.86	43.91	38.22
Y_r	128.63			.039 (1.38)	131.82			0.061+ (1.76)
M_s	43.67	-0.513** (6.85)	-0.549** (7.42)	-0.560** (7.62)	31.41	-0.571** (4.05)	-0.570** (4.39)	-0.658** (4.93)
LF_r	18.02		-0.184* (2.02)	-0.175+ (1.94)	22.37		-0.272* (2.23)	-0.257* (2.20)
F		46.90	27.55	19.49		16.38	12.14	9.95
R^2		.57	.62	.64		.42	.53	.59
Sample size			37				24	
Dependent variable	13.68				19.90			

** Significant at 1 per cent level; * at 5 per cent; + at 10 per cent.

To interpret the partial elasticity coefficient of the growth of the modern sector employment with respect to the rate of growth of the labour force, we reformulate the problem as follows

Let,

the modern sector employment	$= E_o$
the share of the modern sector employment (in the labour force)	$= M_o$
the growth in the modern sector share	$= M^*$
the labour force	$= F_o$
the labour force growth (proportion)	$= L$

Thus by definition $$M_o = \frac{E_o}{F_o} \qquad \ldots 1$$

and the growth in the share of the modern sector employment is given by

$$M^* = \frac{\delta M_o}{\delta \; t}$$

or

$$= \frac{\delta(\frac{E_o}{F_o})}{\delta t} \qquad \ldots\text{substituting from (1)}$$

or

$$= \frac{E_o E'_o - E_o F'_o}{F_o^2} \qquad \ldots 2$$

where E'_o and F'_o are the time derivatives of E_o and F_o respectively.

Now if we impose the condition that the modern sector does not absorb any increased labour supply, then

$$E'_o = 0$$

so that $$M^* = \frac{-E_o F'_o}{F_o^2}$$

but $$F'_o = F_o L$$

therefore $$M^* = \frac{-E_o [F_o L]}{F_o^2}$$

or $$\boxed{M^* = \frac{-E_o L}{F_o}} \qquad \ldots 3$$

Differentiating M* with respect to L, we have

$$\frac{\delta M^*}{\delta L} = \frac{-E_o}{F_o} \qquad \ldots 4$$

Therefore the elasticity of growth in the modern sector share with respect to the labour force growth will be

$$\frac{\delta M^*}{\delta L} \quad \frac{\bar{L}}{\bar{M}^*} = \frac{-E_o}{F_o} \times \frac{\bar{L}}{\bar{M}^*}$$

$$= -M_o \times \frac{\bar{L}}{\bar{M}^*} \quad \text{(since by definition } M_o = \frac{E_o}{F_o}\text{)}$$

or $$\eta_{M^*L} = -M_o \times \frac{\bar{L}}{\bar{M}^*} \quad \text{(where } \eta_{M^*L} = \frac{\delta M^*}{\delta L} \cdot \frac{\bar{L}}{\bar{M}^*}\text{)}$$

Substituting mean value of the variables for the sample of the developing countries, we find

$$\eta_{M^*L} = \frac{-31.41 \times .2237}{19.90}$$

$$= -0.35$$

This is the elasticity coefficient of growth in the share of the modern sector employment with respect to the labour force growth under the condition that the modern sector does not absorb any increased labour supply. And since this observed coefficient is not much different from our estimated coefficient of -0.29, we may conclude that the modern sector did not absorb the increases in the labour force.

The partial elasticity coefficient of growth of the share of the modern sector employment with respect to the level of the modern sector employment (given the rate of growth of the GDP and the labour force) for the sample as a whole (-1.79) as compared with the larger corresponding elasticity for the developing countries alone (-1.04) indicates that the growth in the share of the modern sector employment is likely to be more rapid in the case of the developing countries. This is because the developed countries have already attained higher levels of the modern sector employment so that further increases in the share of the modern sector employment are less probable.

The analysis presented here suggests that since a large proportion of the labour force in the developing countries is currently engaged in agriculture and other traditional sectors, and the rate of growth of the labour force is so high that even with the most optimistic projections of the modern sector growth, all the increases in the labour force cannot be absorbed in the modern sector. The policy implications are, therefore, clear, and well known. But these need to be pursued more rigorously than has been the case in the past. If the employment problem in the developing countries is to be manageable, more labour-intensive techniques of production should be used in the modern sector.[1] Second, efforts should be made to raise the levels of productivity and incomes in the traditional sectors. This would generate a new demand for the modern sector goods and create an additional factor in the shift away from the traditional employment. And finally, the wages should not be allowed to increase disproportionately in the modern sector. Many studies have recently argued that the factor price distortions due to, for example, a rapid upward drift of wages in the modern sector while the various policies cheapening capital through different forms of capital subsidy (e.g. zero or only nominal duties on capital imports, low-interest payments on capital borrowings, etc.), have been

---

[1] For an excellent discussion of the choice of appropriate technologies as instruments of employment and income distribution, see, for example, A.S. Bhalla (ed.): <u>Technology and employment in industry</u> (Geneva, ILO, 1975).

responsible for the low growth rates of the modern sector employment.[1]

VI. Wage-employment and Level and Structure of Exports

Among other factors, the size and the structure of exports have a direct influence on the growth of the modern sector employment. It is hypothesised that the share of the modern sector or wage-employment in the total employment is a positive function of the value of exports, and that the shift from the traditional to the modern sector employment may be greater when the growth in exports is accompanied with changes in the composition of exports. Our indicator of the structure of exports is a statistical composite measure of the extent to which countries have shifted from the exports of the primary products and raw materials to the exports of processed and manufactured commodities.

Separate regressions were run for 1960 and 1970, using the whole sample, as well as a sample of the developing countries.[2] The data for primary and non-primary exports in 1960 and 1970 were compiled from

---

[1] See, for example, Lloyd G. Raynolds: "Wages and employment in a labour surplus economy", in American Economic Review, Vol. 55, No. 1, March 1965; Henry J. Bruton: "Economic development and labour use: a review", in World Development, Vol. 1, No. 12, Dec. 1973; A.D. Witte: "Employment in the manufacturing sector of developing economies: a study of Mexico and Peru", in Journal of Development Studies, Vol. 10, No. 1, Oct. 1973.

[2] All countries with GDP per capita less than $700 were included in the group of developing countries.

the Year Book of International Trade Statistics.[1] The following equation was estimated by ordinary least squares, using the log linear specification.

$$\log X_i = a + b \log ({}^{Y}/N) + c \log ({}^{E}/Y) + d \log ({}^{Em}/E) + e$$

where

X_i = the percentage modern sector and/or wage-employment

$({}^{Y}/N)$ = the GDP per capita in US dollars (at constant price)

$({}^{E}/Y)$ = the percentage share of exports in the GDP

$({}^{Em}/E)$ = the percentage manufactured or non-primary exports

e = the error term

---

[1] (i) For some countries the data did not actually correspond to 1960 and 1970. In such cases, the data available for the closest to these two years were selected. (ii) The primary exports were defined as the sum of items 0-4 given in the revised standard international trade classification (which includes food and live animals, beverages and tobacco, mineral fuels, lubricants and related materials, animal and vegetable oils, fats, etc.) with the exception of manufactured food, beverages and tobacco manufactures, synthetic fibres, synthetic rubber and waste and scrap of primary commodities, refined petroleum and petroleum products, manufactured gas or electric energy, hydrogenerated oil, etc.

The independent variables were introduced stepwise and the regression results are presented in tables 9 and 10.

The regression analysis provides some interesting results. For example, when all countries are included in the sample, the regressions for 1960 indicate that the level of exports (measured as a percentage of the GDP) has a significant relationship with the share of modern sector and/or the wage-employment ratio. But this variable fails to be significant at a 5 per cent level when only a sample of the developing countries is considered (see column 1 in tables 9 and 10). However, for 1970, the level of exports is significantly related to the modern sector and the wage-employment ratio for both the total sample and the sample of the developing countries.

The elasticities of the share of the modern sector employment with respect to the growth of the GDP per capita and the share of exports is greater for the developing countries.[1] For example, in the case of developing countries, a 1 per cent increase in the share of exports in GDP would lead to a 0.48 per cent increase in the share of the modern sector employment in the total employment. By contrast, for the entire sample, the corresponding increase is only 0.23 per cent (see column 2 in table 9). Similarly, the elasticity of the wage-employment ratio with respect to the growth of exports is 0.36 for the developing countries as compared with 0.18 for the sample as a whole (see column 2 in table 10). The larger impact of a given increase in exports on the wage-employment ratio at the lower levels of development is probably due to the adoption of less capital-intensive techniques of production in export industries. It is also interesting to note that the 1970 elasticity coefficients are consistently higher than the corresponding elasticities for 1960. This is perhaps due to the structural changes that have taken place in the composition of exports (see table 11) during this period.

---

[1] The comparison does not include the elasticity of the modern sector employment with respect to exports for 1960, since it was insignificant at the 5 per cent level.

Table 9: Stepwise regression of share of modern sector employment in total employment on GDP per capita, non-primary exports, and share of exports in GDP
(t values are given in brackets)

Independent variables	1960			1970		
	Column 1			Column 2		
Equation	I	II	III	I	II	III
All countries						
Constant	-0.162	-0.398	-0.358	0.161	0.013	0.015
Log ($^{Y}/N$)	.637** (8.92)	.649** (9.46)	.608** (7.83)	.498** (9.02)	.454** (9.00)	.460** (7.69)
Log ($^{E}/Y$)		.173* (2.15)	.160* (1.97)		.234** (3.49)	.235** (3.45)
Log ($^{Em}/E$)			.062 (1.10)			-0.012 (0.17)

/continued...

Table 9 (continued)

Independent variables	1960			1970		
	Column 1			Column 2		
F	79.61	45.75	31.07	81.29	57.86	37.66
R^2	.665	.701	.710	.664	.743	.743
D.W. statistics			1.78			2.25
Sample size	42			43		
<u>Developing countries</u>						
Constant	-1.208	-1.172	-1.203	-0.410	-0.442	-
Log ($^Y/N$)	1.081** (6.96)	1.031** (6.42)	1.022** (6.23)	0.722** (3.73)	.528** (2.76)	-
Log ($^E/Y$)			0.049 (0.50)		.484* (2.33)	-
Log ($^{Em}/E$)		0.072 (1.14)	0.067 (1.02)			

/continued...

Table 9 (continued)

Independent variables	1960			1970		
	Column 1			Column 2		
F	48.39	25.11	16.34	13.92	11.62	-
R^2	.641	.658	.662	.465	.607	-
D.W. statistics			1.98		2.85	-
Sample size		29		18		

** Significant at 1 per cent level; * at 5 per cent.

Table 10: Stepwise regression of wage-employment ratio on GDP per capita, percentage non-primary exports, and share of exports in GDP
(t values are given in brackets)

Independent variables	1960			1970		
	Column 1			Column 2		
Equation	I	II	III	I	II	III
All countries						
Constant	.672	.531	.567	.692	.581	.596
Log ($^{Y}/N$)	.390** (5.63)	.397** (5.75)	.362** (4.61)	.366** (7.00)	.333** (6.61)	.381** (6.25)
Log ($^{E}/Y$)		.103 (1.27)	.091 (1.12)		.176** (2.63)	.178** (2.71)
Log ($^{Em}/E$)			.054 (0.95)			-0.098 (1.59)

/continued...

Table 10 (continued)

Independent variables	1960			1970		
	Column 1			Column 2		
F	31.65	16.88	11.53	49.03	31.54	22.68
R^2	.441	.464	.476	.544	.611	.635
D.W. statistics			2.08			1.51
Sample size	42			43		
<u>Developing countries</u>						
Constant	0.167	0.201	0.171	-0.462	-0.485	-0.492
Log $(^Y/N)$	.605** (3.38)	.558** (2.99)	.549** (2.88)	.836** (5.36)	.692** (4.39)	.795** (4.76)
Log $(^E/Y)$			0.048 (0.41)		.358$^+$ (2.08)	.280 (1.62)
Log $(^{Em}/E)$		.068 (.92)	0.063 (.82)			-0.122 (1.48)

/continued...

Table 10 (continued)

Independent variables	1960			1970		
	Column 1			Column 2		
F	11.41	6.10	4.00	28.73	19.53	14.80
R^2	.297	.319	.324	.642	.722	.760
D.W. statistics			1.90			1.37
Sample size	29			18		

** Significant at 1 per cent level; * at 5 per cent; + at 10 per cent.

Table 11: Share of exports in GDP and percentate non-primary exports*

	Low income countries		Medium income countries		High income countries	
	1960	1970	1960	1970	1960	1970
Percentage share of exports in the GDP ($^E/Y$)	17	17	33	27	21	22
Percentage non-primary exports ($^{Em}/E$)	20	31	39	55	60	68

* These are unweighted mean percentages. E = exports; Em = non-primary or manufactured exports; Y = GDP.

The percentage share of exports in the GDP for low income countries was approximately 17 per cent for both 1960 and 1970. The group II countries had a much higher share of exports in GDP in 1960 which declined in 1970 from 33 to 27 per cent.[1] But there was also a significant shift from the primary to the non-primary exports both for low and medium income countries. For example, the share of the non-primary exports in the total exports increased from 39 to 55 per cent for group II countries.

[1] This does not necessarily mean a decline in exports, but may simply mean that the rate of growth of GDP was faster than the rate of growth of exports during this period.

It is also interesting to note that the share of exports in GDP has a greater effect on the share of modern sector employment than that on wage-employment. On comparing tables 9 and 10, we observe elasticities of 0.23 for all countries, and 0.48 for the developing countries, for the modern sector employment; and corresponding elasticities of 0.18 and 0.36 for wage-employment. Since the modern sector employment includes all professionals, administrative and clerical workers and not just wage-earners, the growth in exports not only generates wage-employment, but also self-employment elsewhere in the economy. These self-employed may be traders or businessmen, supplying several services for the export industry, such as packing, transport and the carriage of goods.

Our analysis indicates that the growth in exports is positively related to a rise in the wage-employment ratio. Our data, however, do not substantiate the other hypothesis that shifts from the traditional to the modern sector employment are greater when the growth in exports is accompanied with changes in the composition of exports. The variable, percentage non-primary exports, fails to be significant in almost all the regressions, particularly when considered together with the other independent variables. This may be partly attributable to the capital-intensive technological changes that usually accompany a shift from the traditional to the manufactured exports. As a result, the independent effect of this variable in raising the share of wage-employment in the total employment is greatly reduced.

Nonetheless, Lydall in his recent study demonstrated that the developing countries should expand manufactured and semi-manufactured exports, as the resulting employment effects will be extensive.[1] The growth in manufactured exports would generate new opportunities for employment in the developing countries

---

[1] See H.F. Lydall: "Employment effects of trade expansion", in International Labour Review (Geneva, ILO), March 1975.

outside the traditional sectors and a continuous shift of the labour force towards the modern sector. However, these observations require further study on the effect of changes in the composition of exports on the shift from the traditional sector employment to the modern sector employment.

VII. Urbanisation and the Modern Sector Employment

The shifts in the sectoral composition of the labour force, and the rural-urban distribution of the population are closely related. The pattern of demand of the urban population is generally biased in favour of the modern sector commodities, and the income elasticity of demand for these products is generally greater than that for agricultural commodities. Therefore, the increasing urbanisation and the rising income levels would lead to an increase in the share of modern sectors in the gross domestic product and, thereby, shift employment to the modern sector activities.[1] On the supply side, urbanisation through the spread of education and the transformation of economic and cultural aspirations would alter the occupational distribution of the labour force from the traditional occupations to the modern sector occupations.[2]

The data in table 12 indicate a general relationship between development and the modern sector employment, on the one hand, and the modern sector employment and

---

[1] See, for example, K.L. Gupta: "Development patterns: an inter-regional study", in Quarterly Journal of Economics, Vol. LXXXV, Nov. 1971.

[2] Urbanisation is associated with a number of changes, such as the growing monetisation of the economy, the spread of education and the transformation of economic and cultural aspirations. See, for example, Vatsala Narain: Demographic aspects of urbanisation Bombay, International Institute of Population Studies, 1975; mimeographed).

Table 12: Modern sector employment, urban population and dependency ratios at different levels of economic development for 1970

Group*	Percentage modern sector employment	Percentage urban population	Child dependency ratio**
1	15.8	14.4	50.6
2	27.3	38.4	44.8
3	36.0	54.9	42.1
4	52.6	62.5+	35.5
5	59.8	64.7	28.0
6	70.3	71.5	27.5

* Countries are grouped on the basis of the GDP per capita in US$ in 1970. Group 1: 1-199; group 2: 200-399; group 3: 400-699; group 4: 700-1299; group 5: 1300-1999; group 6: 2000 and above.

** (Pop. 0-15 x 100)/total population

\+ Hong Kong and Malta are excluded.

urbanisation, on the other. The percentage of the labour force in the modern sector, and the proportion of the urban population vary positively with the level of per capita income. Although the broad associations between these three variables are indicated by the data, in order to establish the degree of relationship we have estimated the following model:

$$\log M_s = a + b \log U + c \log ({}^{Y}/N) + d \log ({}^{E}/Y) + e$$

where

M_s = the percentage modern sector employment (1970)

U = the percentage urban population (1970)

$(^Y/N)$ = the GDP per capita in US dollars (1970)

$(^E/Y)$ = the percentage share of exports in the GDP (1970)

e = the error term

Among the independent variables, the GDP per capita is included because the assumption of a single, well-defined relation between the modern sector employment and urbanisation is not necessarily justified. This relationship may vary according to the level of development.[1] The percentage share of exports in the GDP has already been shown to be significantly related to the share of the modern sector in the total employment in Section VI. Two other variables are also relevant, the size of the market and the child dependency ratio. The size of a country's total population or the labour force can be used as a proxy for the potential size of its internal market.[2] But since the dependent variable

---

[1] The correlation between the percentage urban population and percentage modern sector employment is 0.50 for the developed countries compared with 0.80 for the developing countries. This shows that the association between urbanisation and the modern sector employment is not stable, but varies for different levels of urbanisation and economic development.

[2] It is to be expected that the size of a country's population will affect its pattern of growth. At low levels of development, wider market available to

has been normalised by the size of the labour force, this variable is not included explicitly among the independent variables. The other variable, child dependency ratio, failed to be significant because of its collinearity with GDP per capita and was therefore omitted from the final estimations.[1]

Although the regression results presented in table 13 confirm the over-all positive relation between the modern sector employment and urbanisation, the problem of determining causation still remains. This is because there is an inter-relationship between the growth of the modern sector, on the one hand, and the rising urbanisation and income levels, on the other. The modern sector growth generates employment and affects expectations regarding the future income. These factors, in turn, raise the levels of urbanisation and income.

---

larger countries contributes to earlier and more rapid industrialisation because it enhances the possibilities for capturing both the internal economies of scale and the external economies associated with expanding markets. The large base, therefore, provides a more elastic market, enabling the economy to be inward-looking; see, for example, I. Adelman and C. Morris, op. cit., p. 105.

1 As shown in table 12, the developing countries are characterised by a high percentage of children under 15 years of age, constituting between 42 and 50 per cent of the total population. A high proportion of children implies a heavy dependency load. Families with large numbers of children are likely to be less able to save, and as a result, the level of investment and industrialisation is likely to be lower. When a large proportion of national investment is provided by the government, high fertility is likely to reduce the government's capacity to raise money for investment through taxation. Countries with a high child dependency ratio must also divert a large proportion of the investment funds to social programmes, and this impedes the growth of industrialisation.

Table 13: Stepwise regression of modern sector employment on urban population, GDP per capita, and share of exports in GDP for 1970
(t values are given in brackets)

Independent variables	Regression coefficients		
Equation	I	II	III
Constant	-.007	-.170	-.212
Log U	.953** (10.80)	.593** (5.34)	.544** (5.23)
Log ($^{Y}/N$)		.265** (4.37)	.240** (4.12)
Log ($^{E}/Y$)			.151** (2.50)
F	116.62	91.37	70.79
R^2	.726	.810	.835
D.W. statistic			2.31
Sample size		46	

** significant at 1 per cent level

Conversely, the rising urbanisation and income levels increase the demand for the modern sector goods and induce a further growth in the modern sector. To the extent that urbanisation is determined by the growth in the modern sector employment, our results may be biased. However, many studies have concluded that the growth of urbanisation in the recent past has been faster than the growth of demand for labour in the modern sector, and appears to have been determined increasingly by the expected income.[1] Nevertheless, further research is required to take into account the diversity of these relationships.

VIII. Summary and Conclusions

The main objective of this study was to provide a comprehensive description of the nature and determinants of structural changes in employment that occur during the process of economic development, and examine the implications of these changes for a developing economy.

The major causes of structural changes in employment are to be found in the changing composition of demand and supply of outputs. The low income elasticity of demand for food and primary products implies a shift in demand away from these goods as the level of income rises, whereas the demand for manufactured goods and services will account for an increasing proportion of income. Changes in the composition of production, together with available technology, determine changes in the demand for labour. Factors affecting the supply of labour include the growth of population, its distribution between rural and urban areas and the levels of education.

The analysis based on the international cross-section and time-series data indicates characteristic patterns of change in the sectoral distribution of the labour force and wage-employment. The process of industrialisation and economic development alters the labour force status distribution in favour of wage-employment (i.e. the proportion of self- and family-employment diminishes) in each economic sector, as well as in

---

[1] M.P. Todaro: "A model of labour migration and urban unemployment in less developed countries", in <u>American Economic Review</u>, Vol. 59, March 1969; also see, J.R. Harris and M.P. Todaro: "Urban unemployment in East Africa: an economic analysis of policy alternatives", in <u>East African Economic Review</u> (Nairobi), Vol. 4, 1968.

the economy as a whole. There is also a tendency for the labour force to shift to the sectors of economic activity, characterised by high wage-labour requirements. The secondary and tertiary wage-employment tend to rise, whereas the primary wage-employment declines in relative importance with economic development. However, the data indicate that during the early stages of economic development, the decline of wage-employment in the primary sector is absorbed mainly in tertiary employment, with a smaller effect on the secondary employment. The tendency for the growing proportions of the labour force to be employed in the tertiary sector is largely due to its low elasticity of factor substitution, its slow rate of technological growth and the rapid expansion of economic and social infrastructure in the early stages of economic development. But once a certain stage of development has been reached, the tertiary sector's share in the over-all wage-employment stabilises and declines somewhat, whereas the wage-employment in the secondary sector continues to rise since at the higher levels of development, the demand for manufactured goods grows faster and accounts for an increasing proportion of income.

The distribution of wage-employment by major economic sectors indicates that irrespective of the level of economic development attained, tertiary employment accounts for the largest proportion of wage-employment. The expansion of economic and social infrastructure in the early stages of economic development induces a rise in tertiary employment.

Wage-earners, as a proportion of total employment in each occupation, tend to rise with economic development. The rise is most significant for those occupations characterised by high training and educational requirements. And those occupational groups (white-collar workers) that indicate the high-quality labour content in an economy are precisely the same categories that assume importance with industrialisation and economic development.

In the process of economic development, the relationship between the occupational and industrial distribution of the labour force is also modified as a result of increasing diversity of occupational specialisation within industries, reflecting the growing complexity of economic organisation and technology. Further study on the occupation-industry relationship is required to determine the factors which affect employment opportunities in various occupations, including the effects of the changing technology and shifting demand on the products of various industries.

The application of regression analysis to the available data has shown that the rate of growth of labour force is inversely related to the rate of growth of the share of modern sector employment, given the rate of growth of income and the initial distribution of the labour force between the modern and the traditional sectors. The results also suggest that a high rate of growth of population and the labour force in the developing countries, together with the high initial proportion of the labour force in the traditional sectors, makes it rather unlikely that the growth in the modern sector employment can absorb the total increase in the labour-supply. The relatively slow growth of the modern sector employment in the developing countries between 1960 and 1970 may have been due to the slow growth in demand for the modern sector goods, the adoption of capital-intensive techniques and the high wage-rates. However, the policy implication of these results is clear. If the employment problems in the developing countries are to be manageable, less capital-intensive techniques of production should be used in the modern sector and efforts should be concentrated on raising the levels of productivity and incomes in service and other traditional sectors. This would generate a new demand for the modern sector goods and create an additional factor in the shift away from the traditional employment. Furthermore, most service sectors are, by definition, relatively more labour-intensive. The expansion of this sector in the early stages of economic development (especially for group I countries) is, therefore, potentially an important means of employment-creation.

Our analysis also shows that the modern sector employment is a positive function of the share of exports in GDP. However, the available data fail to substantiate the hypothesis that a shift from the traditional to the modern sector employment is greater when the growth in exports is accompanied with a shift from the exports of primary products and raw materials to the exports of processed and manufactured commodities. Nevertheless, the results do suggest that the expansion of the labour market as a result of increase in foreign trade, not only generates new opportunities for employment in the developing countries but also induces a continuous shift of the labour force status in favour of wage-employment.

We have also observed that the shifts in the sectoral composition of the labour force and the rural-urban distribution of population are closely related. Among other factors, the increasing urbanisation and the rising levels of income, through changes in the pattern of demand, lead to an increase in the share of modern sectors in the gross domestic product, and thereby shift employment to the modern sector activities. On the supply side, urbanisation alters the occupational distribution of the labour force through the spread of education and the transformation of economic and cultural aspirations. Although the regression results confirm the over-all positive relation between the modern sector employment and urbanisation, the problem of determining causation still remains. This is because there is an inter-relationship between the growth of modern sector employment, on the one hand, and the rising urbanisation and income levels, on the other. Further research is required to take into account the diversity of these relationships.

There are other factors which have not been emphasised here but may be considered important in varying circumstances as the determinants of the level and structure of wage-employment. These may include the size of natural resources in a country, the type of political authority, its social institutions, etc. Likewise, there is the question of income distribution and its probable effects on wage-employment levels and structure.

Nevertheless, some broad conclusions have been drawn in this study, using aggregative data. These statistics may be subject to a number of limitations, such as gaps in coverage, and differences in the definitions and classifications adopted in different countries. With international standard industrial and occupational classifications, considerable improvement has been made in the quality and comparability of these classifications, but numerous deviations from the standards still persist. But in spite of the defects of the statistics, it is clear that the proportionate shares of industry, occupation and status groups differ in characteristic ways among countries at different levels of economic and social development.

Appendix A

The wage-employment ratio

The data on wage-employment both for 1960 and 1970 are taken from table 2A of the ILO Year Book of Labour Statistics, for various years. The format of table 2A is given below:

		Employers and workers on own account	Salaried employees and wage earners	Family workers	Other and status unknown	Total
0	Agriculture, forestry and fishing	a_{11}	a_{12}	a_{13}	a_{14}	a_1
1	Mining and quarrying	a_{21}	a_{22}	a_{23}	a_{24}	a_2
2-3	Manufacturing	a_{31}	a_{32}	a_{33}	a_{34}	a_3
4	Construction	a_{41}	a_{42}	a_{43}	a_{44}	a_4
5	Electricity, gas, water and sanitary services	a_{51}	a_{52}	a_{53}	a_{54}	a_5
6	Commerce	a_{61}	a_{62}	a_{63}	a_{64}	a_6
7	Transport and communication	a_{71}	a_{72}	a_{73}	a_{74}	a_7
8	Services	a_{81}	a_{82}	a_{83}	a_{84}	a_8
9(a)	Persons seeking work for the first time	a_{91}	a_{92}	a_{93}	a_{94}	a_9
(b)	Unemployed					
(c)	Activities not adequately described					

The wage-employment ratio is defined as the sum of salaried employees and wage-earners, divided by the total economically active population.

i.e.

$$W^* = \frac{\sum_{i=1}^{8} a_{i2}}{\sum_{i=1}^{8} i_1} \times 100$$

Since for some countries, the breakdown of 'unemployed' and 'activities not adequately described' by job status was not available, these were excluded from the calculations to achieve a greater degree of comparability in data.

The modern sector employment

The percentage modern sector employment and occupational distribution of wage-employment are estimated from table 2B (ILO, Year Book of Labour Statistics) which gives the distribution of economically active population by occupation and job status. The format of table 2B is given below:

		Employers and workers on own account	Salaried employees and wage-earners	Family workers	Other and status unknown	Total
0	Professional, technical and related workers	b_{01}	b_{02}	b_{03}	b_{04}	b_0
1	Administrative, executive and managerial workers	b_{11}	b_{12}	b_{13}	b_{14}	b_1
2	Clerical workers	b_{21}	b_{22}	b_{23}	b_{24}	b_2
3	Sales workers	b_{31}	b_{32}	b_{33}	b_{34}	b_3
4	Farmers, fishermen, hunters, loggers and related workers	b_{41}	b_{42}[1]	b_{43}	b_{44}	b_4
5	Miners, quarrymen and related workers	b_{51}	b_{52}	b_{53}	b_{54}	b_5
6	Workers in transport and communications	b_{61}	b_{62}	b_{63}	b_{64}	b_6
7-8	Craftsmen, production workers and labourers	b_{71}	b_{72}	b_{73}	b_{74}	b_7
9	Service, sport and recreation workers	b_{81}	b_{82}[1]	b_{83}	b_{84}	b_8

/continued...

	Employers and workers on own account	Salaried employees and wage-earners	Family workers	Other and status unknown	Total
10 (i) Workers not classified by occupation	b_{91}	b_{92}[2]	b_{93}	b_{94}	b_9
					$\sum_{i=0}^{8} b_i = B$

[1] Since the professional, administrative and clerical workers have already been included, the residual wage-employment in agriculture is predominantly composed of labourers in traditional agriculture. These two categories, although in wage-earning employment, are usually subject to traditional working conditions and are, therefore, excluded from the calculations of the modern sector employment.

[2] Again for some countries, the lack of breakdown of this group by job status led to the exclusion of this group from the calculations to achieve a greater degree of comparability in the data.

The percentage modern sector employment is defined as

$$m^* = \frac{m_1^* + m_2^*}{B} \times 100$$

where m* is the percentage of the total employment in the modern sector.[1]

---

[1] An attempt is also made to systematically exclude the armed forces, thus restricting the definition of the modern sector employment to civilian employment.

$m_1^* = (b_0 + b_1 + b_2)$ is the sum of all professional, administrative and clerical workers (both wage-earners and self-employed)

$M_2^* = (b_{32} + b_{52} + b_{62} + b_{72})$ is the sum of wage-earners among sales, mining, transport and production process workers

and B = the economically active population.

Appendix B

GDP per capita

GDP per capita is taken from the UN *Statistical Year Book* (1973), the UN *Year Book of National Accounts Statistics* (1972), and the UN *Monthly Bulletin of Statistics* for various years. For some countries, the 1960 figures actually correspond to the 1963 figures.

Population

Population figures have been drawn from the following sources:

(i) UN *Demographic Year Book* (various years)

(ii) UN *Statistical Year Book for Asia and the Far East* (1972)

(iii) UN *Population and Vital Statistics Report, Series A, Vol. XXVI, April and July 1974*

(iv) OECD *Labour Force Statistics, 1961-79* (Paris, 1974)

Urban population

The urban population figures for 1960 are from the UN *Department of Economics and Social Affairs Report No. ESA/P/WPS*, 1970; and for 1970 from the UN *Population and Vital Statistics Report*, statistical papers Series A, Vol. XXVI, No.2, April 1974; and the UN *Demographic Year Book* (1972).

The sources of data for other variables, such as the primary and non-primary exports, and the rate of growth of the labour force, have been defined in the text at appropriate places.

Appendix C

Classification of countries by GDP per capita in 1960

Group I (GDP per capita less than US$ 300 in 1960)

Country	1960	1970
Nepal	72	85
India	74	97
Thailand	97	183
Egypt	129	214
Sierra Leone	140	177
Sri Lanka	142	174
Republic of Korea	152	260
Morocco	154	216
Angola	169	292
Ghana	198	257
Iran	203	392
Syria	209	307
Liberia	223	357
Dominican Republic	238	363
Seychelles[1]	-	246
Algeria	248	324
Colombia	253	409
Nicaragua	254	431
Guatemala	274	367
Portugal	281	631
Chile	294	684

[1] 1960 observations are not available.

Group II (GDP per capita greater than US$ 300 but less than US$ 700 in 1960)

Country	1960	1970
Mexico	334	682
Spain	341	957
Hong Kong	348	745
Costa Rica	370	544
Martinique	384	828
Panama	392	731
Malta	410	718
Greece	418	1094
Lebanon	426	533
Singapore	432	950
Japan	462	1911
Argentina	623	1078
Ireland	635	1322

Group III (GDP per capita greater than US$ 700 in 1960)

Country	1960	1970
Italy	701	1726
Puerto Rico	787	2009
Austria	891	1938
Israel	939	1884
Finland	1116	2213
Belgium	1232	2651
Norway	1277	2932
Denmark	1299	3170

Group III (continued)

Country	1960	1970
Germany, Fed. Rep.	1300	3049
France	1336	2889
United Kingdom	1359	2139
Bahrain[1]	-	1367
New Zealand	1559	2195
Australia	1586	2932
Sweden	1861	4090
Canada	2229	3874
Kuwait	4902	3995

---

[1] 1960 observations are not available.